THE PAGAN ORIGINS OF CHRISTIAN HOLIDAYS

ELISHA J. ISRAEL

THE PAGAN ORIGINS OF CHRISTIAN HOLIDAYS.
Copyright © 2013 Elisha J. Israel. All rights reserved.
Printed in the United States of America. No part of this
book may be used or reproduced in any manner
whatsoever without written permission except in the
case of brief quotations embodied in critical articles and
reviews. All rights reserved.

Visit www.elishajisrael.com

DEDICATION

To my father

CONTENTS

SUNDAY: DAY OF THE S-U-N NOT THE S-O-N	2
JANUARY 1: HONORING THE GOD OF NEW BEGINNINGS	20
VALENTINE'S DAY: REMNANT OF A DARK LOVE	24
CARNIVAL "FAREWELL TO FLESH"	29
LENT: AWAITING THE REBIRTH OF SPRING	33
EASTER (ISHTAR)	38
TRINITY SUNDAY: THREE GOD PRINCIPLE CONTINUES	50
CORPUS CHRISTI: "EATING THE GOD"	58
HALLOWEEN: THE CELTIC NEW YEAR (SAMHAIN)	64
THE SEASON OF ADVENT ("THE COMING" OF THE PAGAN GOD)	72
ON DECEMBER 25TH A SUN IS BORN	75
SHINING THE LIGHT ON EPIPHANY	93
FEASTS IN HONOR OF THE QUEEN OF HEAVEN	101
GOD IS A SPIRIT	111
BIBLIOGRAPHY	114

God is a Spirit: and they that worship him must worship him in spirit and in truth.

- John 4:24

NOTE TO READER

If you are like me you grew up celebrating holidays like Christmas and Easter. Some of my favorite memories were from these celebrations. Waking up on Christmas morning to open gifts that Santa left, and dressing up on Halloween was fun for me as a child. But, while in college at the age of about twenty something happened. I started to read the bible, and I mean intensely. And the more I read and read one thing became abundantly clear. Practically everything concerning God that I had learned in the Christian Church, and in my Catholic prep school contradicted the Holy Bible. I then began to consider all those joyous celebrations that I loved as a child, and my mind became bombarded with questions. Questions like what does a Christmas tree have to do with Jesus? Why do people have Easter egg hunts in commemoration of the resurrection of Christ? Why do Christians celebrate Halloween? That is a high day for witches! Where exactly did Valentines day come from? After much study, I came to realize that practically every Christian holiday is rooted in paganism. After reviewing the historical and biblical evidence presented in this book it will one thing will become unequivocally clear. It is a grave contradiction to believe in the God of Abraham, Isaac, and Jacob and simultaneously celebrate Christian holidays.

1
SUNDAY: DAY OF THE S-U-N NOT THE S-O-N

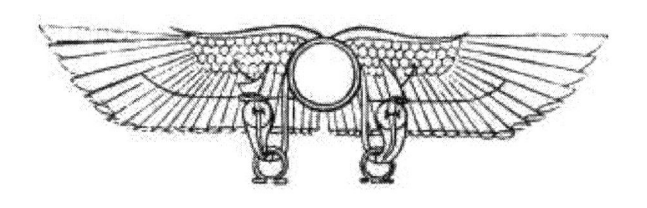

"If I had to choose a religion, the sun as the universal giver of life would be my god."
-Napoleon Bonaparte

Sunday is the first day of the week. Many millions of self-professing Christians set aside Sunday as a day to reverence God. It is considered to be the analogue of the Seventh Day Sabbath. Some even refer to Sunday as the "Christian Sabbath" or the "Lord's Day". However, the sanctification of Sunday can in no way be substantiated with the Holy Bible. Rather, it can be traced back to the time of antiquity during which men worshipped the sun as God, the source and sustainer of life on the earth.

The Pagan Origin of Sunday Worship

Throughout human history sun worship has been almost universal. The sun has been revered throughout time as the giver and sustainer of life. *In The Secret Teachings of the Ages* Manly P. Hall writes:

> To them (aboriginal peoples) he (the sun) was the innate fire of bodies, the fire of Nature. Author of Life, heat, and ignition, he was to them the efficient cause of all generation for without him there was no movement, no existence, no form. He was to them immense, indivisible, imperishable, and everywhere present. It was their need of light, and of his creative energy, that was felt by all men; and nothing was more fearful to them than his absence. His beneficent influences caused his identification with the Principle of Good; and the Brama of the Hindus, and Mithras of the Persians, and Athom, Amum, Phtha, and Osiris, of the Egyptians, the Bel of the Chaldeans; the Adonai of the Phoenicians, and the Adonis and

Apollo of the Greeks, became but personifications of the Sun, the regenerating Principle, image of that fecundity which perpetuates and rejuvenates the world's existence.[1]

The sun was personified and worshiped throughout the world under many names. And Sunday, or the day of the Sun, has been and continues to be the foremost pagan day of worship. Originally, sun worship was based on the sun and the six known planets. By the time of the Roman imperial period the days of the week were named in honor of these pagan gods:

> Day of the Sun- dies Solis
> Day of the Moon- dies Lunae
> Day of Mars- dies Martis
> Day of Mercury- dies Mercuii
> Day of Jupiter- dies Iovis
> Day of Venus- dies Veneris
> Day of Saturn- dies Saturni

The current days of the week were named in honor of Roman and Germanic deities[2]:

> Sun- Derived from Latin

---

[1] Manly P. Hall, *The Secret Teachings of the Ages: An Encyclopedia Outline of Masonic, Hermetic, Qabbalistic adn Rosicrucian Symbolical Philosophy* (San Francisco: H.S. Crocker Company, Inc. 1928), 119.
[2] Norse is an Old Germanic language.

Monday- Derived from Latin
Tuesday- Originally Tiwesdaeg 'Day of Tiw", from the Norse Tysdagr
Wednesday- Originally Wodnesdaeg 'day of Woden (Odin)
Thursday- Originally Thursdaeg 'day of Thor, from Norse Thorsdagr
Friday- Originally Frigesdaeg 'day of Freya' from the Norse Freyjasdagr
Saturday Derived from the Latin

The first civil or ecclesiastical law sanctioning Sunday worship was put forth by Constantine on March 21, 321 A.D. This edict reads:

> On the venerable Day of the sun let the magistrates and people residing in cities rest, and let all workshops be closed. In the country, however, persons engaged in agriculture may freely and lawfully continue their pursuits: because it often happens that another Day is not suitable for grain sowing or for vine planting: lest by neglecting the proper moment for such operations the bounty of heaven should be lost.[3]

Many attribute this edict to the "conversion" of Constantine I that is traditionally associated with his victory over Maxentius in 312. However, throughout his reign Constantine retained the title of Pontifex Maximus[4], and continued to refer to the

---

[3] *Codex Justinianus*. Lib. 3, tit, 12, 3.
[4] Latin for "Greatest Pontiff", the most prestigious position in the College Pontificum (college of pontiffs) in Ancient Rome.

first day of the week as dies solis (the day of the sun) and the Sol Invictus (Invincible Sun). It is most probable that in his effort to strengthen his empire he utilized Christianity because of its potential future unifying elements throughout the peoples of the Roman Empire.[5] Rulers, both secular and religious, followed suit in authorizing Sunday worship, which turned a pagan practice into a Christian ordinance. For example, in 386 A.D. Theodosius I and Gratian Valentinian put forth laws that restricted litigation as well as payments of public and private debt on Sunday. One of the most influential of these edicts was put forth by the Catholic Church Council of Laodicea. The Council of Laodicea declared:

> Christians shall not Judaize and be idle on Saturday (Sabbath), but shall work on that Day: but the Lord's Day, they shall especially honour, and as being Christians, shall, if possible, do no work on that Day. If however, they are found Judaizing, they shall be shut out from Christ.

Gibbons maintains that the Catholic Church and Constantine made concessions with paganism in order to achieve certain objectives. He writes:

The Pontifex Maximus served as the head of the pagan Roman religion.

[5] Aleksander Aleksandrovich, *History of the Byzantine Empire, 324-1453 Vol. 1* (Madison: University of Wisconsin, 1952), 49.

...it must ingenuously be confessed, that the ministers of the Catholic church imitated the profane model, which they were impatient to destroy. The most respectable bishops had persuaded themselves, that the ignorant rustics would more cheerfully renounce the superstitions of paganism, if they found some resemblance, some compensation, in the bosom of Christianity. The religion of Constantine achieved, in less than a century, the final conquest of the Roman Empire: but the victors themselves were insensibly subdued but the arts of their vanquished rivals.[6]

The prominence of Sun-worship throughout the Roman Empire is why Sunday was sanctified by the Universal Church. Understand, from Genesis to Revelation there is no commandment to sanctify the first day of the week. Nevertheless, various Christian denominations utilize two arguments to justify Sunday worship in honor of God. The most popular argument used to uphold Sunday worship is that it is the day Jesus was resurrected from the grave. The second, is that Sunday worship was observed weekly in the New Testament instead of the Seventh Day Sabbath as is commanded throughout the Old Testament. Both arguments are easily refuted.

---

[6] Edward Gibbon *The History of the Decline and Fall of the Roman Empire* (London: Oxford University, 1837), 449.

3 Days and 3 Nights

The first position that Jesus was resurrected on Sunday is used as the justification of Easter observance as well as Sunday veneration is flawed because the Messiah was not resurrected on Sunday. The common doctrinal teaching is that Jesus was crucified on Friday (Good Friday) and rose on Sunday (Easter). However, this is impossible based on Jesus' own words. In the Matthew 12 it is written:

> Then certain of the scribes and of the Pharisees answered saying, Master, we would see a sign from thee. But he answered and said unto them, An evil and adulterous generation seeketh after a sign; and there shall no sign be given to it, but the sign of the prophet Jonas: **For as Jonas was three days and three nights in the whale's belly; so shall the Son of man be three days and three nights in the heart of the earth.**[7]

The profession of Jesus disproves the widely accepted doctrine that He died on a "Good" Friday. If Jesus died on Friday it means that He only spent one day and two nights in the sepulcher.

---

[7] Matthew 12:38-40.

1 Day and 2 Nights Theory to Support Sunday Resurrection

"Good Friday" Night

Saturday Day   Saturday Night

> According to tradition, Jesus was resurrected on Sunday, which is used to justify Easter observance.

According to the Bible, Jesus actually died on the Passover which fell on a Wednesday of that week, and was resurrected on the Sabbath (Saturday) of the same week. This fact is recorded by Matthew who writes, "And it came to pass, when Jesus had finished all these sayings, he said unto his disciples, **Ye know that after two days is the feast of the passover, and the Son of man is betrayed to be crucified.**"[8] We know that by the time the first day of the week came Jesus had already been resurrected from the grave. This is why when Mary came to the sepulcher she assumed that someone had taken the body of Jesus. Understand, she came

---

[8] Matthew 26:1-2. *See also* Mark 14:1-2 & Luke 22:1-2.

at the beginning of the first day, when it was yet dark. John reads:

> The first day of the week cometh Mary Magdalene early, **when it was yet dark**, unto the sepulchre, and seeth the stone taken away from the sepulchre. Then she runneth, and commeth to Simon Peter, and to the other disciple, whom Jesus loved, and saith unto them, They have taken away the Lord out of the sepulchre, and we know not where they have laid him.[9]

3 Days and 3 Nights (Matthew 12:38-40)

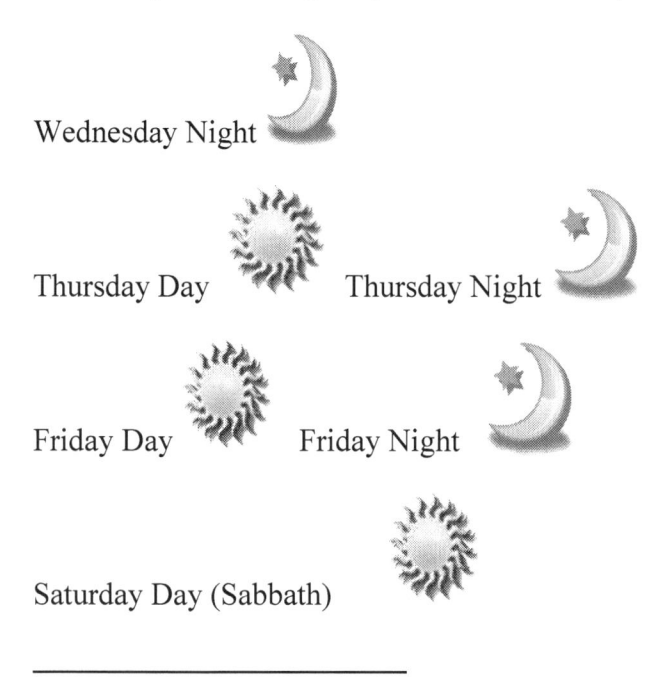

Wednesday Night

Thursday Day   Thursday Night

Friday Day   Friday Night

Saturday Day (Sabbath)

---

[9] John 20:1-2.

> According to the Holy Bible Jesus died on the Passover, which fell on a Wednesday, and was resurrected from the dead on the Sabbath (Saturday) of the same week.

Weekly Sunday Convocations in the New Testament?

Many Christians claim that Sunday convocations were sanctioned in the New Testament. What all those who profess to be Christians should understand is that from Genesis to Revelation one will not find a commandment to sanctify Sunday instead of the Sabbath Day.[10] We must bear in mind that Jesus Christ, the one who Christians claim to follow, did not hold a holy convocation on Sunday. In Luke it is written, "And he came to Nazareth, where he had been brought up: and, as his custom was, he went into the synagogue on the sabbath day, and stood up for to read." Paul also had the same custom. Luke goes on to write, "Now when they had passed through Amphipolis and Apollonia, they came to Thessalonica, where was a synagogue of the Jews: And Paul, as his manner was, went in unto them, and three sabbath days reasoned with them out of the scriptures." Those who still hold fast to Sunday

---

[10] The annual Feast of Pentecost, or Feast of Weeks falls every year on the first day of the week. (See Leviticus 23:15-16). This is the only time during which we are commanded to hold a holy convocation specifically on the first day of the week.

worship should consider that Paul honored not only the Seventh Day Sabbath but after the death and resurrection of Christ he still observed the annual feast days of the Lord as well.[11] These days were not "nailed to the cross" as some may profess. And how could they be? The Lord's feast days are a shadow of things to come. The word "Sabbath" means rest and the Seventh Day Sabbath points to the 1000 years of peace during the Millennium Period. When one understands the significance of the Sabbath it makes the notion of Sunday worship that much more objectionable.

Some utilize the writings of Paul to argue that holy gatherings were held on Sunday. For this purpose, Acts 20:7 is often used. It reads as follows, "And upon the first day of the week, when the disciples came together to break bread, Paul preached unto them, ready to depart on the morrow; and continued his speech until midnight." Prior to leaving on his journey Paul simply preached the Gospel unto some on the first day of the week. But one should not read Acts 20:7 and conclude that we are to now gather every Sunday instead of on the Sabbath. Others maintain that Paul was indeed preaching on the Sabbath and discourse simply carried on into the next day. Nevertheless, one should consider why Paul was determined to sail by Ephesus, as is stated in the following verses. He was determined to be in Jerusalem for Pentecost.[12] Are we to believe that Paul was observing the annual feasts of God as is commanded but had

---

[11] *See* Acts 20:6-7, 16.
[12] *See* Acts 20:16.

established Sunday worship which is not commanded? Furthermore, what are we to make of his custom, which was to honor the Sabbath? Considering the chapter in context sheds light on what the truth is. The truth is that those who want to maintain that Sunday worship is desired by God are either truly misinformed or are being untruthful. Some maintain after citing this verse that we can worship God every day to justify replacing the Sabbath with Sunday. But the issue is not if we should worship God every day. The question is concerning what day God commands us to cease from our labors and hold an holy convocation. If we look to the Bible for the answer we can only conclude that it is the Seventh Day Sabbath. Another lesser used reference to substantiate Sunday convocations is found in I Corinthians, "Upon the first day of the week let everyone of you lay by him in store, as God hath prospered him, that there be no gatherings when I come."[13] But this in no way sanctions Sunday observances. Paul simply desired that the collection be taken up for the brethren at Jerusalem occur prior his arrival.

Catholic Proclamation Concerning Sunday Worship

Those of the Protestant faith who utilize inadequate arguments to substantiate Sunday observance often ignore the fact that the Catholic Church readily admits to sanctioning Sunday worship. *The Faith of Our Fathers*, written by

---

[13] I Corinthians 16:2.

James Cardinal Gibbons and considered to be one of the best explanations of Catholic doctrine, clearly states that there is not one single line in the Holy Bible authorizing Sunday sanctification. Gibbons maintains that throughout the Scriptures only Sabbath (Saturday) observance is ordained.[14] The Catholic Church also maintains that through "divine authority" it has changed the Sabbath to Sunday, and the simple fact that they have been able to do so proves this authority. Furthermore, Sunday worship among Protestants is one of the major arguments against the Protestant Reformer's cry of "Sola Scriptura".[15] Archbishop Reggio D. Daspare de Fosso of Calabra responded to this cry as follows:

> The Protestants claim to stand upon the written word only. They profess to hold the Scriptures alone as the standard of faith. They justify their revolt by the plea that the Church has apostatized from the written word and follows tradition. Now the Protestants claim, that they stand upon the written word only, is not true. Their profession of holding the Scripture alone as the standard of faith, is false. PROOF: The written word explicitly enjoins the observance of the seventh day as the Sabbath. They do not observe the seventh day, but reject

---

[14] James Gibbons, *The Faith of Our Fathers: Being a Plain Exposition and Vindication of the Church Founded by Our Lord Jesus Christ* (New York: John Murphy Company Publishers, 1917), 89.

[15] Latin for "by scripture alone".

it. If they do truly hold the scripture alone as their standard, they would be observing the seventh day as is enjoined in the Scripture throughout. Yet they not only reject the observance of the Sabbath enjoined in the written word, but they have adopted and do practice the observance of Sunday, for which they have only the tradition of the Church. Consequently the claim of 'Scripture alone as the standard,' fails; and the doctrine of 'Scripture and tradition' as essential, is fully established, the Protestant themselves being judges.[16]

The question posed by some Catholic scholars is quite compelling. How could Protestants profess to take their religion solely from the Holy Scriptures and observe Sunday instead of honoring the Sabbath as the Bible commands? On the other hand, just as troubling is the Catholic Church's profession that they have been given divine authority to institute Sunday worship. God has given no man authorization to violate His word. Both Catholics and Protestants who observe Sunday worship should consider what the Holy Bible states concerning the altering of God's word. Deuteronomy 4 reads, "Ye shall not add unto the word which I command you, neither shall ye

---

[16] Heinrich Julius Holztmann, *Kanon und Tradition: ein Beitrag zur neueren Dogmengeschichte und Symbolik* (Ludwigsburg, Germany: F. Reihm, 1859), 263.

diminish ought from it, that ye may keep the commandments of the Lord your god which I command you."[17]

---

[17] Deuteronomy 4:2.

James Cardinal Gibbons (1834-1921)

Baptism of Constantine as imagined by the students of Raphael (1520-1524)

THE PAGAN ORIGINS OF CHRISTIAN HOLIDAYS

Excavated slab depicting Sol Invictus (Artist Unknown, 150-200 B.C.)

2
JANUARY 1: HONORING THE GOD OF NEW BEGINNINGS

On the modern Gregorian calendar January 1 is celebrated as the initial day of the new year. Because the vast majority of the world has adopted the Gregorian calendar, New Year's Day is considered the only global public holiday. Around the world this celebration is commemorated by shooting fireworks and rounds of ammunition into the midnight sky. January 1 has been incorporated into the Catholic Church as well as the Eastern Orthodox Church. However, celebrating this date as the beginning of the new year was established from a pagan perspective. To find the origins of this pagan holiday we need but only to look at ancient Rome.

In 46 Julius Caesar, with the assistance of the Egyptian astonomer Sosigenes of Alexandria, revised the previously used calendar and established the new year in January. However, this particular calendar was quite unsound. For instance, the year 46 B.C., often referred to as the "Year of Confusion", had 445 days and fifteen months. On February 24, 582, Pope Gregory XIII introduced the calendar which is utilized throughout most of the known world today.

The month January was named in honor of Janus, the god of new beginnings, gates, and doors. In early Rome prior to the use of statues to represent their gods, the Romans worshiped Janus as a doorway. This is similar to how Vesta was considered "naught else but living fire."[18] Representations of Janus had two faces, one looking forward to the future and the other gazing backwards into the past. To Caesar it was appropriate for the new year to be in this month because it would be the "doorway" to the new year. In honor of Janus Romans engaged in banqueting and licentious sexual activities.

---

[18] Bessie Rebecca Burchett, *Janus In Roman Life and Cult: A Study in Roman Religions* (Menasha, Wisconsin: George Banta Publishing, Co., 1912), 27.

January 1, Not Only Pagan But Also Arbitrary

When we consider God's creation one must understand that the change or transition in seasons, and days, and years is observable. In Genesis 2 it is written:

> And God said, Let there be lights in the firmament of the heaven to divide the day from the night; and let them be for signs, and for seasons, and for days, and years: And let them be for lights in the firmament of the heaven to give light upon the earth: and it was so. And God made two great lights; the greater light to rule the day, and the lesser light to rule the night: he made the stars also. And God set them in the firmament of the heaven to give light upon the earth. And to rule over the day and over the night, and to divide the light from the darkness: and God saw that it was good.[19]

So according to what God has established, at evening begins a new day, a new moon is the beginning of a new month, and a new year begins in the spring when everything in nature is regenerated.

But according to man's calendar, the new year begins at 12:00am on January 1. This date and time is totally arbitrary. We should ask the question, "What is new in the dead of winter"? In nature things are new in the springtime. When God delivered the children of Israel from Egyptian bondage He told Moses and Aaron, "This month

---

[19] Genesis 1:14-18.

shall be unto you the beginning of months: it shall be the first month of the year to you."[20] This was the month Abib which corresponds to the spring months of April and May.

In their usual manner of attempting to make holy that which is vile, the Roman Catholic Church up until 1969 maintained that January 1, was the day that Jesus was circumcised. The Eastern Orthodox Church still holds the position that Jesus was circumcised on the first day of January. Chapter 11 entitled, "On December 25th a Sun is Born" explains that Jesus could not have been born on December 25 and consequentially was not circumcised on January 1. Nor is Mary the "mother of God" (*see* Chapter 13 "Feasts in Honor of the Queen of Heaven").

---

[20] Exodus 12:2.

3
VALENTINE'S DAY: REMNANT OF DARK LOVE

"Neither potent herbs, nor prayers, nor magic spells shall make of thee a mother, submit with patience to the blows dealt by a fruitful hand."

-Publius Ovidius Naso (Latin poet, 43 B.C.- 17 A.D.)

It is likely that Valentine's Day, a day that is associated with love and romance, was birthed out of the ancient Roman feast Lupercalia (February 13-15). Lupercalia was celebrated annually in honor of Lupercus, Pan, and Juno Februata (Juno the fructier).[21] The day February 15 was called dies februatas (the day of expiation or purification) and the month februarius was known as the month of

---

[21] Cora Linn Morrison Daniels and Charles McClellan Stevens *Encyclopedia of Superstitions, Folklore, and the Occult Sciences of the World* (Milwaukee, WI.: J.H. Yewdale & Sons Co., 1903), 1536.

purification. This festival of Lupercalia was officiated by the luperci. The luperci was a minor college divided into two colleges, Luperci Quinctiales or Quinitilli and the Luperci Fabiani or the Fabii. During this festival, the priests of Luperci would come together in the cave of Lupercal on Palatine Hill where according to legend the founders of Rome Romulus and Remus were nursed as infants by a lupa or she-wolf. On Palatine Hill every February 15, the Luperci sacrificed animals known for their strong sexual instinct, such as goats (the Lupercal) and dogs (Faunus), to the god of fertility. Two sons of noble distinction were then chosen and anointed with the bloody sacrificial knife upon their foreheads. Milk soaked wool was then wiped on the young boys at which time they began to laugh. Subsequently, the goat's were cut into thongs called *februa* and the boys ran throughout the city scantly covered with goat hides striking women with the thongs. Ovid offered four reasons for the boys nakedness: The Greek god Pan himself runs naked 2.285-88, the primitive Arcardians who worshipped Pan did not wear clothes 2.289-302, the Roman god Faunus dislikes clothes because of sexual contretemps caused when Hercules and Omphale exchanged clothes 2.303-58, at a feast for Faunus, Romulus and Remus and their followers were exercising in the nude when they had to rush off, still undressed, in pursuit of cattle rustlers 2.361-80.[22]

It was believed that such a strike would aid in

---

[22] Ovid, Betty Rose Nagle, *Ovid's Fasti: Roman Holidays* (Bloomington, IN: Indiana University Press, 1995), 8.

conception and childbirth, thus women of rank received these lashes willingly. An allusion to this custom is found in Shakespeare's *The Tragedy of Julius Caesar:*

> Caesar: Calphurnia!
> Calphurnia: Here, my lord.
> Caesar: Stand you directly in Atonius' way When he doth run his course. Antonius!
> Anotinius: Caesar, my lord?
> Caesar: Forget not, in your speed, Antonius, To touch Calphurnia; for our elders say, The barran, touched in this holy chase, Shake off their sterile curse.[23]

It should be noted that it was during this feast in 44 B.C that Julius Caesar was offered the crown three times by Mark Antony who was the high priest of the Luperci.

---

[23] William Shakespeare, *The Dramatic Works of William Shakespeare, with a Glossary* (London: H.G. Bohn, 1858), 852.

Caesar Refuses the Diadem of kingship offered by Marc Antony, 44 B.C.

Later, the Romans began a licentious love lottery in which young men drew the names of young women from an urn. The two were paired together and became sexual partners for a period of time. The lover's lottery was also very popular during Medieval England.

Like many secular festivals Lupercalia was given a Christian cloak. In 496 A.D. Pope Gelasius I replaced the licentious pagan Lupercalia with a festival in honor of the martyr Valentine. However, there is debate concerning exactly which Saint Valentine Gelasius was referring to. There was a Valentine in a Roman province in Africa and

Bishop Valentine of Interamma (modern day Terni, Italy). However, the most popular candidate was a bishop in Rome during the reign of Claudius. During his reign Claudius the Cruel engaged Rome in many bloody military campaigns. He viewed marriage as a hindrance to military victory and banned the religious sacrament. According to legend, Bishop Valentine of Rome continued to perform marriages and as a consequence was beheaded by Claudius. In some versions of the legend, during his imprisonment Valentine converted members of his jailer's family to Christianity, and prior to his execution sent a farewell letter to the jailer's daughter that was signed "From your Valentine". Gelasius made Valentine the patron saint of love and chose the date of his death (February 14th) as the day to commemorate his life. Over time the Lupercalia was replaced with St. Valentine's Day. Eventually, it became customary for lovers to exchange gifts and messages on this day. However, the sexual wanton behavior that occurred during the ancient Lupercalia festival still persists within the current celebration of Valentine's Day.

4
CARNIVAL "FAREWELL TO FLESH"

Carnival is the time before the Lenten season. It is a popular festival celebrated largely in Catholic countries. The origin of the name "Carnival" is disputed by scholars. It is possible that the word "carnival" comes from two Latin words "carne" and "vale". Carne means "flesh" and vale means "farewell". This would signify the last days that meat could be consumed before Lent. Some scholars see similarities between Carnival and the Roman festival of the Navigium Isidis (Ship of Isis).[24] During this festival a parade of masks followed an adorned boat with a statue of Isis was carried to the shore in order to bless the new sailing season.

Carnival probably derived from ancient pagan pre-spring festivals of the Greeks and Romans. The ancient Greeks held feasts in honor of Dionysus the god of wine, pleasure, and fertility. Romans observed the Bacchanalia festival in honor Bacchus, the god of wine and pleasure. Lupercalia was held in honor of Lupercus, who guarded the flocks. Sacrifices were also offered to Faunus the goddess of fertility and woodlands. There was also Saturnalia which upturned the societal hierarchy. During this homage to Saturn slaves became masters and peasants were given autonomy. Just like the pagan festivals of old Carnival is inundated with gluttony, drunkenness, and sexual debauchery. Perhaps the anonymity provided by the Carnival mask influenced the excessive amount of sexual license.

The sexual licentiousness of this time could not be Christianized, nor could these carnivals be stamped out by the Roman Church. Perhaps the medieval Feast of Fools, during which partiers held a mock mass and impersonated Catholic Church officials, indicates the Roman's Church failure get rid of the carnival. Eventually, however,

---

[24] Maximilian Josef Rudwin, *The Origin of the German Carnival*, (New York, G.E. Stechert & Co.,1920), 6.

Throughout Europe, Carnival was adopted by the Catholic Church and was connected to Lent. Carnival spread throughout the world through European colonization.

Today, Carnival is celebrated throughout Central and South America, the Caribbean, as well as in parts of Africa. Mardi Gras (Fat Tuesday) was brought to North America by The French explorer Pierre Le Moyne D'Iberville who on March 2, 1699 (Luna Mardi Gras) led a party up the Mississippi River. On March 3, 1699 (Mardi Gras Day) D'Iberville set up camp on what is today Plaquemines Parish, Louisiana. He named the location *Point du Mardi Gras* (Mardi Gras Point) in honor of the festival. In 1702, Jean Baptiste Le Moyne de Bienville found Mobile Alabama. The following year French settlers there began celebrating Mardi Gras. Although, New Orleans is most well known for its Mardi Gras celebrations many historians believe that the first Mardi Gras in America took place in Mobile, Alabama. Today, peoples throughout the world where Carnival has been introduced have added their own twist to the celebration. However, it is common, practically wherever you find Carnival, for people to engage in drunkenness, sexual voyeurism, fornication, prostitution, and homosexuality similar to the pagans of old. Therefore, how could it be justifiable to link such a celebration to Christianity?

Procession in Honor of Isis (Navigium Isidis Festival)

5
LENT: AWAITING THE REBIRTH OF SPRING

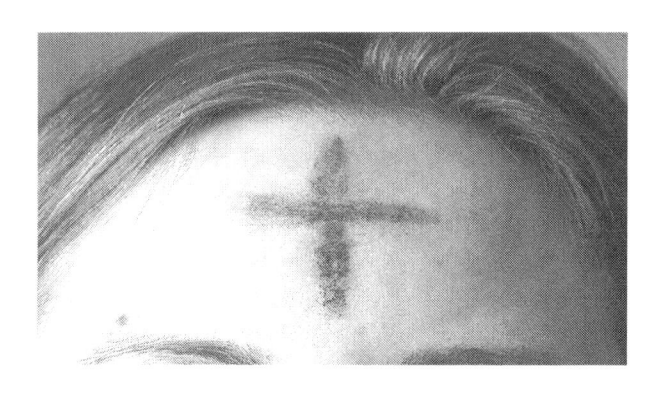

"It ought to be known that the observance of Lent did not exist, as long as the primitive church retained its perfection unbroken."
- Cassianus, 5th Century

Lent is the "fortieth" day before Easter and is observed in many Christian denominations. This is the six and one half week period that lasts from Ash

Wednesday to Easter Sunday. During Lent Christians fast and refrain from various pleasures. This is said to be for the purpose of preparing to commemorate the passion, death, and resurrection of Christ.[25] Although the Holy Scriptures do ordain a period of fasting in commemoration of the passion of Christ, this was not the forty day period known as Lent. In the Book of Leviticus it is written, "And the Lord spake unto Moses, saying, Also on the tenth day of this seventh month there shall be a day of atonement: it shall be an holy convocation (holy gathering) unto you; and ye shall afflict your souls (fast) ..."[26] Furthermore, Paul prophesied of such a doctrine concerning unholy fasting in his epistle to Timothy. I Timothy reads as follows:

> Now the Spirit speaketh expressly, that in the latter times some shall depart from the faith, giving heed to seducing spirits, and doctrines of devils; Speaking lies in hypocrisy, having their conscience seared with an hot iron; **Forbidding to marry, and commanding to abstain from meats**, which God hath created to be received with thanksgiving of them which believe and know the truth.

Paul is specifically prophesying of the rise of the Catholic faith. In Catholicism, which is the mother

---

[25] Some Christian denominations associate this fast with the 40 day fast that Jesus endured in the wilderness prior to being tempted by Satan. This is justified despite the fact that this was a total fast and had no relation to Easter.
[26] Leviticus 23:26-27.

of all other Christian denominations, priests are prohibited from getting married. In addition, they have instituted a spring fast and attributed it to the suffering of Christ. However, such a fast and its rituals are rooted not in Christ but in the pre-Christian pagan worship of antiquity.

The word Lent means "spring" and derived from the Old English word "Lencten". Spiritually speaking, all roads lead to Babylon and such is the case in regard to forty day spring fasts. In one version of the Babylonian myth, Tammuz the great hunter was slain while hunting a wild boar. Devotees mourned for him through weeping ceremonies for forty days. During the days of Ezekiel this ritual was even found among the Israelites. Ezekiel writes:

> He said also unto me, Turn thee yet again, and thou shalt see greater abominations that they do. Then he brought me to the door of the gate of the Lord's house which was toward the north; and behold, there sat women **weeping for Tammuz**.

Worshippers of Tammuz wept with his consort Ishtar believing that his rebirth would mean the regeneration of life within nature. Similar feasts are found throughout pagan peoples of antiquity. For instance, the ancient Egyptians observed a forty day fast in honor of Osiris. The sign of the cross rubbed with ashes is not exclusive to Constantinian Christianity; it is found throughout the ancient world and was used as a prominent symbol of the pagan Gods. For example, "the Tau cross was inscribed on the foreheads of initiates into the Mysteries of Mithras." It is also interesting to note that the act of simply sprinkling ashes directly on the head, which is also done on Ash Wednesday, was done in honor of the pagan Norse god Odin as well. The placing of ashes above the brow always occurred on Wednesday, the day named in honor of Odin.

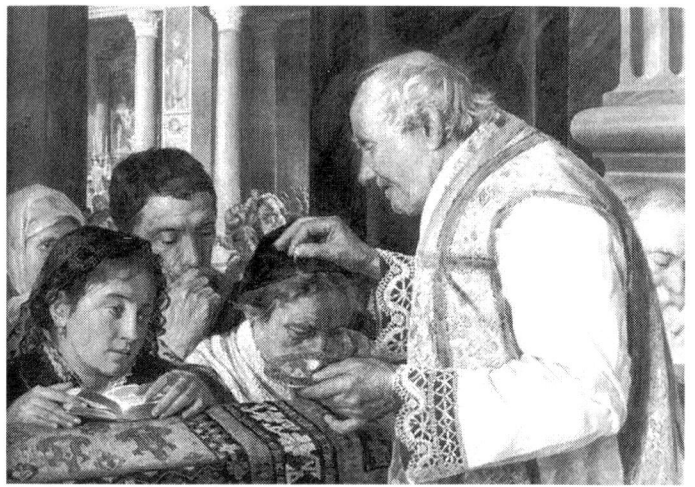

Catholic priest sprinkles ashes on the head of parishioners

If it is true as Cassianus attests that, "...the observance of Lent did not exist, as long as the primitive church retained its perfection unbroken"27 why is it observed today? Within the Holy Scriptures we find no commandment to observe such a fast. Undoubtedly, if the Christian

---

[27] John Cassian, *Conference 21, The First Conference of Abbot Theonas on the Relaxation During the Fifty Days*, Chapter 30.

veneer of Lent is wiped away, we see what mirrors an ancient pagan fast.

6
EASTER (ISHTAR)

Easter is perhaps the most prominent festival in the Christian religion. It is a moveable feast that occurs on the Sunday after the vernal equinox. According to Christian tradition Easter Sunday is the festival that commemorates the resurrection of Christ on the third day. However, as has already been mentioned in a previous chapter (*see* "Chapter

1 Sunday: Day of the S-U-N Not the S-O-N"), Christ could not have possibly been crucified on Friday and resurrected on Sunday. The only sign that Jesus gave to indicate that He was indeed the Christ was that He would be in the grave for three days and three nights.[28] Just like that, the justification for celebrating the most important holiday in the Christian faith is disproven. It is also just as effortless to illustrate the pagan underpinning of this cherished solemnity.

Origin of the word "Easter"

In Acts 12:4 we find the only instance of the word "Easter" in the Bible. However, the word was translated from the Greek word "Pascha" which means "Passover". When read in context it becomes clear that Luke is not referencing the time of Easter as Christian tradition proclaims. Acts 12 reads, "And because he saw it pleased the Jews, he proceeded further to take Peter also. (Then were the days of unleavened bread)."[29] Passover is the day of preparation for the Feast of Unleavened Bread. The word "Easter" actually derives from the Anglo-Saxon goddess Eostre. She is identified with the Babylonian fertility goddess Ishtar.

Sexual Rituals in honor of Ishtar (Easter)

In Babylon, like many other ancient pagan cultures, human sexuality was associated with

---

[28] *See* Matthew 12:38-40.
[29] Acts 12:3.

fertility in nature. Temples were erected in Ishtar's honor and sexual ritualism was associated with the worship of her. Some scholars attest that each year around the time of the spring equinox the marriage of Ishtar and her consort Tammuz was reenacted. This ceremony consisted of a sexual ritual between the king of Babylon and the high priestess of Babylon. It was believed that this union would ensure plentiful crops. Sacred prostitution was also practiced in honor of Ishtar. Herodotus describes this lascivious act as follows:

> The foulest Babylonian custom is that which compels every woman of the land to sit in the temple of Aphrodite (Ishtar) and have intercourse with some stranger once in her life. Many women who are rich and proud and disdain to mingle with the rest, drive to the temple in covered carriages drawn by teams, and stand there with a great retinue of attendants. But most sit down in the sacred plot of Aphrodite, with crowns of cord on their heads; there is a great multitude of women coming and going; passages marked by line run every way through the crowd, by which the men pass and make their choice. Once a woman has taken her place there, she does not go away to her home before some stranger has cast money into her lap, and had intercourse with her outside the temple; but while he casts the money, he must say, "I invite you in the name of Mylitta". It does not matter what sum the money is; the woman will never

refuse, for that would be a sin, the money being by this act made sacred. So she follows the first man who casts it and rejects no one. After their intercourse, having discharged her sacred duty to the goddess, she goes away to her home; and thereafter there is no bribe however great that will get her. So then the women that are fair and tall are soon free to depart, but the uncomely have long to wait because they cannot fulfill the law; for some of them remain for three years, or four. There is a custom like this in some parts of Cyprus;.[30]

There were also homosexual male prostitutes known as *assinnu*, *kurgarru*, and *kulu'u*. These devotees of Ishtar were castrated and engaged in lifelong service of men in honor of Ishtar.

Intermingled Symbols and Practices of Pagan Worship

Easter Eggs

In addition to the name, the symbols associated with the Easter festival also reveal its pagan influence. In paganism the mundane egg is symbolic of the manifestation of the cosmos. The egg is also a symbol of rebirth that is associated with various pagan deities. The ancient Egyptians

---

[30] Herodotus and Alfred Denis Godley, *The Histories Vol. 1* (London: William Heineman, 1920), 1.199.

hung eggs in their temples.[31] Seb, the Egyptian god of time supposedly laid an egg, "...at the time of the great one of the Dual Force". In the ancient Greek Orphic tradition the primordial hermaphroditic god hatched from an egg and then created the deity. Among the Phoenicians the Agathodæmon embraced the mundane egg. The Chinese believed that when the earth was in total darkness that Poon-Koo-Wong sprang from an enormous egg as a human being with tremendous powers.[32] According to one Babylonian legend an egg containing Ishtar fell from heaven and landed in the Euphrates River. This cosmic egg of wondrous size was pushed to shore by fish and incubated by a dove. In Babylon we also find the roots of Easter eggs hunts. Colored eggs were also used in honor of Ishtar.[33] And, ancient pagans believed that finding "Ishtar's egg" in nature at the time of her rebirth would bring forth a blessing. In ancient Anglo-Saxon mythology the fertility goddess Ostara changed her bird into an egg laying hare. These brightly colored eggs were given as gifts to children. After the rise of Christianity the egg became a symbol of the tomb from which Christ was resurrected, and Christians continued the pagan custom of painting eggs during the festival of Easter.

---

[31] James Bonwick, *Egyptian Belief and Modern Thought* (London: London: Paul & Co., 1878), 211-212.
[32] William Chambers, Robert Chambers, W & R Chambers, *Chamber's Journal of Popular Literature, Science and Arts* (London: W & R Chambers, 1894), 160.
[33] Helena Pretrovna Blavatsky, *The Theosophical Glossary* (New York: Theosophical Publishing Society, 1892), 110.

THE PAGAN ORIGINS OF CHRISTIAN HOLIDAYS

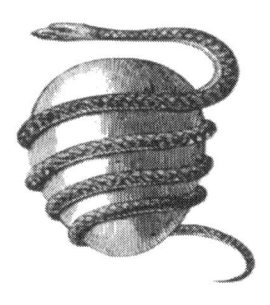

The Orphic Egg

Easter Egg Roll on White House South Lawn 1929

Hares

In paganism the rabbit is a sign of sexual fertility, fecundity, and the moon. A rabbit or hare has four to eight litters each year. During its lifespan a rabbit can potentially produce up to six hundred offspring. It was believed that hares had sex indiscriminately and were thus associated with the fertility goddesses in whose honor sexually wanton acts were committed. Rabbits were mainly associated with Ostara and Aphrodite. They were sacrificed on the altars and even the consumption of rabbit meat was believed to remedy infertility well into the 17th Century. Two "cures" read as follows:

> "Take of the slime that a hare will have about his mouth when he eateth mallows, and drink it in wine; two hours after lie with your husband... Or, give to the woman without her knowledge the womb of a hare to eat, or burn the same to powder and give it to her in wine."[34]

The hare like Easter is associated with the moon. This nocturnal creature carries her young for a month, the length of the moon cycle. A new moon was considered masculine and the vanishing moon feminine.[35] It was once believed that both the

---

[34] William Sermon, *The Ladies Companion, or the English Midwife*, London, 1671.
[35] William S. Walsh, *Curiosities of Popular Customs and of Rites, Ceremonies, Observances, and Miscellaneous Antiquities*, (Philadelphia: J.B. Lippincott, 1897), 366.

hare and the moon had the ability to change their sex. Aristotle and Pliny both believed that the hare was male one year and female the next. The hare was also a symbol of pagan folklore because it was said that the dark patches on the moon looked like leaping hares.[36]

New Clothing

During Easter it is customary to don a new set of clothing. Pagans also did this around the time of the Equinox in celebration of the Ostara. In the Teutonic pagan tradition it was bad luck to wear spring garments before Ostara. New elegant garments were sewn during the winter to be worn during the spring festival.[37]

Easter Lilies

Lilies are among the flowers associated with the Easter season. The lily is also revered by pagans. Pagans revered the lily and considered the flower to be a phallic symbol because it resembled the male reproductive organ.

Easter Ham

It is tradition amongst many Christians to eat a

---

[36] Raven Grimassi, *Encyclopedia of Wicca and Witchcraft*, (St. Paul, MN: Llewellyn WorldWide, 2000), 203.
[37] Edain McCoy, *The Sabbats: A Witch's Approach to Living the Old Ways* (St. Paul, MN: Llewellyn Publications, 1994), 111.

ham on Easter. This custom may in fact have derived from Babylon. According to legend, Tammuz was killed by a wild boar on a hunting expedition, and Isthar descended into the underworld to rescue him. In her absence He died along with most vegetation. Each year a pig was consumed by the devotees of Ishtar and Tammuz to avenge the death of their sun god.

Hot Cross Buns

Some attest that the hot cross bun derives from the buns that were utilized in the worship of the Ostara.[38] These hot cross buns were initially Equinox cakes marked with a cross, the astrological sign for the Earth and the Earth Mother. Devotees to this goddess believed that by consuming Equinox cakes they could absorb magical powers.[39] Traditionally, these buns were eaten during the Lenten season from Shrove Tuesday until Good Friday, and the meaning of the pagan cross was then associated with the Crucifixion. Jeremiah records that the nation of Israel engaged in a similar practice. In Jeremiah it is written:

> The children gather wood, and the fathers kindle the fire, and the women knead their dough, to make cakes to the queen of heaven, and to pour out drink offerings unto other gods,

---

[38] Reader's Digest, *The Last Two Million Years*, (London : The Reader's Digest Association, 1973), 216.
[39] Cassandra Eason, *A Complete Guide to Night Magic*, (New York: Kensington Publishing Corp., 2003), 193.

that may provoke me to anger.[40]

Easter Fires

Large bonfires set ablaze on the night before Easter (Holy Saturday) and the justification for doing so is that these fires represent the resurrection of Jesus, the light of the world. However, such fires were set long before the observance of the Christian festival known as Easter. Pagans throughout Europe set large fires that represented spring's victory over the winter season. It was believed that these fires chased the cold and darkness away. After several unsuccessful attempts to stamp out this ritual it was simply adopted by the Catholic Church and given a new meaning.

Sunrise Service

Both Catholics and Protestants observe a sunrise service on Easter. After a nightly vigil a worship service is held as the sun rises on Easter Sunday. This custom derives from the ancient spring festivals. During the Vernal Equinox in pre-Christian times pagans celebrated the rising sun. In the book of Ezekiel we read that similar sun worship was practiced by the ancient Israelites. The prophet writes:

> And he brought me into the inner court of the Lord's house, and, behold, at the door of the temple of the Lord, between the porch and the

---

[40] Jeremiah 7:18.

altar, were about five and twenty men, with their backs toward the temple of the Lord, and their faces toward the east; and they **worshipped the sun toward the east**.

Although many Christians take part in this custom in honor of the Resurrection of Christ, it is done in grave error. John tells us that when Mary Magdalene came to the sepulcher in the end of the Sabbath when it was yet dark an angel informed her that Jesus had already risen. Jesus was crucified on the Passover which fell on a Wednesday of that week and was resurrected on the Sabbath (Saturday), not Sunday.

Easter not celebrated by Early Christians

Easter was not a festival that was observed by the Apostles or the early Christians. Even Tertullian asks, "If the Apostles set aside all reference to days and months and years, why do we celebrate Pascha in the first month of each year?".[41] There is no evidence that Easter was observed in the New Testament. Easter in relation to Christ was not celebrated until several hundred years after His death. It was common practice of the Catholic Church to overtake the pagan days and rites in order to lure in the pagans. The pagan Sunday was transformed into the Christian Sunday. Sunday and Easter are identical because Sundays, from the

---

[41] Samuel Macauley Jackson, *The New Schaff-Herzog Encyclopedia of Religious Knowledge*, (New York: Funk & Wagnalls Co., 1909), 43.

Catholic perspective, are simply the reoccurrence of the Easter (Resurrection) Sunday.[42] The obvious problem with such a position is that stamping the name of Jesus on a pagan day does not in reality make the day "Christian". On the contrary, those who observe Easter are simply continuing the pagan customs of antiquity.

---

[42] William L. Gildea, *Paschale Gaudium* in The Catholic World, Vol. LVIII., No. 348. (New York: Office of The Catholic World, March 1894), 808-809.

7
TRINITY SUNDAY: THREE GOD PRINCIPLE CONTINUES

"There is no evidence the Apostles of Jesus ever heard of a trinity"

- H.G. Wells, Outline of History, 1921 Edition, p. 499

Trinity Sunday is a Christian holiday that is observed in the Western Liturgical churches (Catholic, Anglican, Lutheran, Presbyterian, Methodist, and Baptist). In Roman Catholicism the official name for Trinity Sunday is the *Solemnity of the Most Holy Trinity.* Trinity Sunday is a moveable feast that is observed one week after Pentecost Sunday. It is held in recognition of the fundamental belief in the Holy Trinity. This is the belief that God is three persons (Father, Son, and Holy Spirit), each being equal and indivisible. The establishment of this day is rooted in the Arian

Controversy of the 4th Century. Arius (A.D. 256-336), the Presbyter of Alexandria, Egypt, believed that the Father preceded Jesus Christ. Arian and his followers (Arians) believed that the "Son has a beginning, but God has no beginning"[43] and that the Father, Son, and Holy Ghost were separate entities. In 325 AD Emperor Constantine organized the Council of Nicaea which consisted of 318 Catholic bishops who met in Nicaea in Bithynia (Anatolia, modern Turkey). One of the major issues to be resolved was the Christological dispute concerning the Arian question regarding the relationship between the Father and the Son.[44] The Council of Nicaea condemned the teachings of Arias and proclaimed that Jesus was of the same substance as the Father. By this time Constantine had already made Christianity the official state religion so any deviation from the teachings of the Roman Catholic Church was considered to be rebellion against the state. Thus, Arias was excommunicated from the Roman Church and exiled to Illyra (modern Albania).

---

[43] Letter of Arius to Eusebius of Nicomedia, Theodoret, *Church History* 1.5. Eusebius, although a friend of Constantine sympathized with Arian.

[44] Melitian controversy, establish the date of Easter, baptism of heretics.

The Council of Nicaea (325 A.D.)

To strengthen the position of the Trinity doctrine within Catholicism prayers and hymns were composed and recited in Church liturgies as part of the Divine Office. Soon a version of the office was celebrated on the Sunday subsequent to Pentecost. Finally, Pope John XXII (1316-1334) made the celebration of Trinity Sunday universal.[45]

---

[45] Universal means celebrated throughout the Catholic Church.

Pope John XXII

Although presently the doctrine of the Trinity is largely accepted by many Christian denominations, the observance of a day in honor of the Trinity is problematic for several reasons. First, the word "Trinity" is not found in the Old or New Testaments. It was not even formally accepted by the Catholic Church until the 4th Century. Furthermore, it is accepted by both secular and religious scholars alike that the doctrine of the Trinity is not found within the pages of the Holy Scriptures. Even the Catholic Church readily admits that the Trinity is not found in the Holy Bible. So, if the concept of the Trinity is not found in the Holy Scriptures from where did it stem? Like practically every custom, and religious observance of the Catholic Church, it originated from paganism. Edwards Gibbons writes:

> If Paganism was conquered by Christianity, it is equally true that Christianity was

corrupted by Paganism. The pure Deism of the first Christians... was changed, by the Church of Rome, into the incomprehensible dogma of the trinity. Many of the pagan tenets, invented by the Egyptians and idealized by Plato, were retained as being worthy of belief.[46]

Egyptian Trinity (Osiris, Horus, and Isis,)

---

[46] Edward Gibbon, *History of Christianity* (New York: Peter Eckler Publishing Co., 1916), xvi.

Indian Trinity (Brahma, Shiva, and Vishnu)

Depiction of the Chrisitan Trinity, "Dogmatic Sacrophagus"

Since antiquity man has conceptualized God in the form of a trinity or triad. Many scholars trace this to ancient Babylon. In Babylon god was worshipped in the form of Nimrod (Baal or Bel), Semiramis/Ishtar, and Tammuz. According to legend Nimrod was deified and worshipped as God. His wife Semiramis soon was impregnated by the "rays of the sun" (Nimrod) and brought forth the "promised seed" (Tammuz). The Egyptian trinity consisted of Osiris, Isis, and Horus. After the death of Osiris he was supernaturally resurrected so that Isis could become pregnant and bring forth a sun named Horus. Through Horus Osiris was reborn.[47] The concept of the Trinity that originated in Babylon spread throughout the world. For instance, In India we find Brahma, Shiva, and Vishnu in Scandinavia there is Odin, Freya, and Thor, the Greek Olympic triad consists of Zeus, Athena, and Apollo. Within platonic philosophy the demiurgic is comprised of Zeus, Poseidon, and Pluto. For the pagan convert the doctrine of the Trinity was tolerable because it varied from his own concept of God in name only.

---

[47] This is one of many triads found in ancient Egypt (e.g., Amum, Mut, and Khonsu, Ptah, Sekhmet, and Nefertem, Khnum, Satet, and Anuket, and Ra in the form of Kheper, Re-Horakhty, and Atum). There are also Hellenized versions of the Egyptian trinity.

8
CORPUS CHRISTI: "EATING THE GOD"

Corpus Christi, also known as Corpus Domini, is celebrated mainly by Christians, but also by Anglicans, the most notable being the Church of England. Corpus Christi is a moveable feast that falls at the earliest on May 21 and at the latest on June 24. This feast is celebrated on the Thursday after Trinity Sunday or on the Sunday after Holy

Trinity.[48] Corpus Christi literally means "the body of Christ" in Latin. This Latin rite is a celebration of the traditional belief in the pagan Eucharist.

Corpus Christi was promoted largely by Juliana of Liège (ca. 1192-1258) who supposedly at the age of 16 began having almost daily visions of a half-moon with a dark spot. In 1208 she had a vision of Christ during which she was told to plead for the institution of Corpus Christi. She appealed to Jacques Panteleon (Archdeacon of Liège who later became Pope Urban IV). In 1246 a synod was issued and it began to be celebrated. In 1264 Pope Urban IV made Corpus Christi a universal feast throughout the Roman Church.[49] According to legend, this act was inspired by a procession to Orvieto when a priest in Bolsena witnessed a bleeding host. It should be noted that this "Eucharistic miracle" has been called into question by many scholars.

According to the Roman Catholic doctrine of transubstantiation (Latin *transsubstantiatio*, Greek μετουσίωσις *metousiosis*) in the Eucharist, the bread and the wine *literally* transform into the substance of the body and blood of Christ. In other words, Catholics believe that once the Eucharist is consecrated the bread literally becomes the body of Christ and the wine becomes His blood. The Council of Trent (1551) declared:

> Because Christ our Redeemer said that it

---
[48] In countries where Corpus Christi is not an Holy Day of Obligation it falls on the Sunday after Holy Trinity.
[49] *Papal Bull Transiturus de hoc mundo*.

was truly his body that he was offering under the species of bread, it has always been the conviction of the Church of God, and this holy Council now declares again, that by the consecration of the bread and wine there takes place a change of the whole substance of the bread into the substance of the body of Christ our Lord and of the whole substance of the wine into the substance of the bread into the substance of the body of Christ our Lord and of the whole substance of the wine into the substance of his blood. This change the holy Catholic Church has fittingly and properly called transubstantiation.[50]

This doctrine of transubstantiation does not however, derive from what Jesus did on the Passover, or what is commonly referred to as the Last Supper. This practice of "eating the god" is one the oldest practices in the pagan religions.[51] For instance, in ancient Egypt the wheat cakes that were consecrated in honor of Osiris became his flesh and were consumed by his followers. In the mystery religion of Mithras there was also a Eucharist similar to the Catholic rite. This custom was also common in the Americas. When certain Catholic missionaries first arrived in the Americas they observed a religious ceremony that was likened to communion during which devotees ate cakes

---

[50] *Catechism of the Catholic Church, 1376*.
[51] Will Durant, *The Age of Faith: The Story of Civilization Vol. 4*, (New York: Simon and Schuster, 1950), 741.

made of flour and declared that it was the flesh of their god. Prescott writes:

> "Their surprise was heightened, when they witnessed a religious rite which reminded them of communion...an image made of flour...and after consecration by priests, was distributed among the people who ate it...declaring it was the flesh of deity..."[52]

According to the doctrine of transubstantiation the priest has the power of Jesus to summon Him off of the throne of God to the altar to be sacrificed once more. In *The Faith of Millions* John O' Brien stated that the Catholic priest has a power greater than saints, angels, and Mary. The words of the Catholic priests' consecration reach to the throne of heaven and literally call Jesus off of the Father's throne to be slain on the altar for man's sins again. And, once the priest speaks, Christ must bow in humility and is obedient to be sacrificed a thousand times.[53]

Certain aspects of the practice of transubstantiation are identical to that of witchcraft. For instance, in witchcraft the supernatural beings are forcibly brought into subjection by the priest. Similarly, Catholics profess that Jesus has no choice but to submit to the Roman priest and be repeatedly

---

[52] William Hickling Prescott, and John Foster Kirk, *History of the Conquest of Mexico: With a Preliminary View of the Ancient Mexican Civilization, and the Life of the Conqueror, Hernando Cortés, Volume 3* (Philadelphia: J.B. Lippincott & Company, 1882), 369.

[53] John O' Brien *The Faith of Millions* (Huntington, IN: Our Sunday Visitor, 1974), 255-256.

sacrificed. Another common belief among pagans was that the character, physical attributes, and intellectual capabilities of animals and men could be acquired through the consumption of their flesh. Frazer writes:

> The savage commonly believes that by eating the flesh of an animal or man he acquires not only the physical, but even the moral and intellectual qualities which were characteristic of an animal or man; so when the creature is deemed divine, our simple savage naturally expects to absorb a portion of its divinity along with its material substance. It may be well to illustrate by instances this common faith in the acquisition of virtues of vices of many kinds through the medium of animal food, even when there is no pretence that the viands consist of the body or blood of a Jesus. The doctrine forms part of the widely ramified system of sympathetic or homeopathic magic.[54]

Jesus is the ultimate sacrifice, He is the Lamb that was slain from the foundation of the world. However, this sacrifice was only made once, not repeatedly. Furthermore the bread and wine was symbolic of body and blood, not literally apart of him. The Catholic Church has merely replaced the cross with a pagan altar.

---

[54] James George Frazer, *The Golden Bough: A Study in Magic and Religion* (London: Macmillan and Company, 1912), 138-139.

THE PAGAN ORIGINS OF CHRISTIAN HOLIDAYS

Corpus Christ Procession

9
HALLOWEEN: THE CELTIC NEW YEAR (SAMHAIN)

Halloween is an annual holiday that is celebrated in many western countries on October 31. On this day children dress up in costumes and trick or treat from house to house, adults attend costume parties, make jack-o-lanterns, visit haunted houses, have séances, and tell scary stories. Many Christians ignore the obvious ungodly customs of Halloween. Halloween evolved from the Celtic

New Year Samhain (pronounced Sow-en or Sow-in). The Celts lived approximately 2,000 years ago in what is now Great Britain, Ireland, and France (Gaul). To Celts Samhain was the day the life of the sun ceased thus causing summer to end.

It was also believed that during Samhain the veil between the physical and spiritual world was the most thin, and that souls were released from the land of the dead. Druid priests set sacred bonfires on hilltops and sacrificed plants, animals, and humans to the Gaelic deities. Celtic households relit their hearths from the flames of the bonfires. These fires were used to scare away any unwanted spirits. One popular belief was that the dead who had been offended by the living would return to destroy crops or bring about other misfortunes. During this day the Celts also wore costumes and engaged in dances that were symbolic of the cycles of life and death. Many dressed in animal costumes to signify the release of the souls that resided in animals. Masks made of animal heads were adorned to hide from the trickery of feared deities. The priests also attempted to communicate with the dead, and prognosticated using the remains of sacrificed animals.

By 43 A.D. the Romans conquered the Celts, and two autumn festivals of the Romans (Feralia and Pomona's Day) were intermingled with the Celtic feasts. Farelia was observed on February 21. This day signified the end of Parentialia, a nine day feast for the dead. During the feast of Parentialia the Romans made offerings in honor of their deceased family members. At midnight on the

Feraila the heads of each household would speak to the evil spirits and ancestors to ensure their return to the spirit world. If this was done on February 22 the Caristia (Cara Cognatio) feast was held. On this day families feasted together and offered food and incense in honor of Lares. Also, on this day any family quarrels were forgotten. On November 1 the festival of the fertility goddess Pomona (Pomorum) was celebrated. Pomona was the goddess of fruit and trees and was often depicted with apples. This is probably how apples became associated with Halloween. Over time apples were used to divine concerning marriage. When the apple is cut in half, the seeds form a type of pentagram, a symbol that represented fertility to the Celts. Thus it is quite natural that the apple could be used in their divination. This is most likely where the custom of "bobbing" or ducking for apples derived. During this time young unmarried peopled would bob for apples. The first one to bite into an apple would be the first to marry. The divination of the time and fertility of Pomona were combined in the spirit of the Samhain festival.

After the emergence of Christianity Samhain was still observed. To supplant Samhain Pope Boniface IV designated May 13 as All Saint's Day in honor of the dead saints. However, this was not sufficient to completely thwart the deeply entrenched Samhain festival. So in 835 Pope Gregory IV transferred All Saint's Day to November 1. Samhain which was celebrated the night before eventually was called All Hallows Eve and later became Halloween. In 1000 A.D. the

Catholic Church established November 2 (All Souls Day) to honor the dead who were not considered saints.   On All Souls Day it was common for the poor to "go a-souling". This consisted of going door to door and requesting simple pastries called soul cakes; in exchange the poor would pray for the souls of home dweller's dead relatives that were in purgatory. Many believe that this is the origin of trick or treating.

Making jack-o'-lanterns originated from Irish folklore. One common myth was that there was a drunkard named "Stingy Jack". Jack had an infamous reputation for his silver tongue and evil deeds. According to one version of the tale Jack was able to trick the Devil into climbing a tree. He then placed a cross on the tree which prevented the Devil from climbing down. Jack made a deal with the Devil that he would let him down if he would never take his soul. The Devil agreed and Jack removed the cross. When Jack died he was prevented from entering heaven and also barred from hell. Jack had no light to see his way. Mockingly the Devil gave Jack an ember that had been lit with one of the everlasting flames of hell. Jack carved out the inside of a turnip and placed the ember inside of it. He was known as Jack of the Lantern or Jack-o'-lantern. When the Irish migrated to America they brought this custom of making jack-o'-lanterns with them. However, in America pumpkins were more available and replaced the turnip.

The customs that have been associated with Halloween such as witchcraft and sorcery demonstrate that this holiday is antithetical to the word of God. As a matter of fact, Halloween is considered a high day among those who follow the Wiccan religion. If this is the case how can Christians justify observing this festival? In Deuteronomy it is written:

> When thou art come into the land which the Lord thy God giveth thee, thou shalt not learn the abominations of those nations. There shall not be found among you any one that maketh his son or his daughter to pass through the fire or that useth divination, or an observer of times, or an enchanter or a witch, or a charmer, or a consulter with abomination unto the Lord: and because of these abominations the Lord thy god doth drive them out from before thee. Thou shalt be upright with the Lord thy God.[55]

---

[55] Deuteronomy 18:9-13.

Painting of Pomona by Nicolas Fouche' (Circa 1700)

Bonfire during Samhain (Edinburg, 2008)

Icon of Second Coming of Christ with Saints (used for All Saints Day) circa 1700

10
THE SEASON OF ADVENT ("THE COMING" OF THE PAGAN GOD)

The season of Advent begins the liturgical year. This Christian penitential festival is observed during the four Sundays that proceed Christmas. Advent is considered the preparation period for the Nativity of Jesus. The Advent feast was mentioned as early as

380 A.D. at the Council of Saragossa. Advent, A period of intense preparation through prayer and fasting for Epiphany, begins on the fourth Sunday before Christmas (Sunday between November 27 and December 3). Initially, six Sundays were calculated before Christmas, but this period was reduced to four by Pope Gregory the Great. The word "Advent" is an anglicized version of the Latin word "*adventus*" (Parousia), which means "coming", and is of pagan origin.

This time signified the annual arrival or coming of divinities into the pagan temples. During adventus these temples that were usually closed where opened. Often statues of gods and goddesses were moved from small places into much larger areas. During adventus ceremonies it was believed that the deities of veneration dwelled amongst the worshippers. In Ancient Rome, there was also an imperial adventus. The imperial adventus signified the coming of the emperor. The emperor would enter the city, usually with his army after a military victory. In a splendid display of power the emperor would appear in the procession as the new *patronus* for the Roman people. This was one of the rare times during which the people could interact with their emperor. After Constantine passed the Edict of Milan (313), which allowed the practice of the Christian religion, pagan feasts such as adventus were given a Christian twist. During this shift adventus was equated with the advent of the Messiah.

The Advent wreath is a reminder of this intermingling of paganism. The lighting of the

Advent wreath is a long-standing Catholic custom. However, it is most likely that the wreath predates Christian times. The sun was central to pagan worship and held a place of extreme importance in society. Pagans celebrated the year of Yule by lighting large bonfires (Yule log), and torches in honor of the dying sun. To please the sun-god and ensure that he would return during the dark part of the year (Winter Solstice), worshippers would also decorate a cart-wheel with lights and offer it to the Sun. The practice of lighting a wreath was incorporated into Christianity as the religion spread throughout Europe. The rebirth of the sun was supplanted by the birth of the Son of God, but the pagan custom remained.

11
ON DECEMBER 25TH A SUN IS BORN

> Hear ye the word which the Lord speaketh unto you, O house of Israel: Thus saith the Lord, Learn not the way of the heathen, and be not dismayed at the signs of heaven; for the heathen are dismayed at them. For the customs of the people are vain: for one cutteth a tree out of the forest, the work of the hands of the workman, with the axe. They deck it with

silver and with gold; they fasten it with nails and with hammers, that it move not.
                                                            -Jeremiah 10:1-4

Christmas is a "Christian" holiday that is observed in commemoration of the birth of Jesus Christ. This festival is considered a religious as well as a cultural holiday and is celebrated by billions of the earth's inhabitants. During the Christmas season, Christians and non-Christians send gifts to loved ones, acquaintances, and even strangers. However, this anniversary was not celebrated by early Christians, nor is there a decree to commemorate Christ's birth. The important date of Christmas as well as the rites, symbols and figures associated with this festival actually predate Christianity.

Why December 25th?

Why does the "Christian" world celebrate the birth of Christ on December 25th? First and foremost, we find within the laws of God the days that Christians should observe (Seventh Day Sabbath, Passover, Feast of Unleavened Bread, Pentecost, Memorial of the Blowing of Trumpets, Day of Atonement, Feast of Tabernacles, (*See* Leviticus 23). The observance of December 25th, even if it was the birth date of the Messiah is not commanded. Furthermore, a closer look at the account of the birth of Jesus provides insight into the time when Jesus was born. This analysis suggests that the Messiah could not have been born on December 25th for a number of reasons.

Shepherds abiding in the field

Although the exact date of the birth of Christ is not provided by any of the Gospel writers, according to the account of Luke, in Bethlehem there were shepherds abiding in the field at the precise time of Jesus' birth.[56] It was not the custom of the shepherds in this area to abide with their flocks during the winter. Shepherds sent their flocks out to graze and brought them back during the first rains. Winters in Bethlehem during December can be extremely cold and the ground covers with frost or snow. This is especially true during winter nights when winds are piercingly cold.

Jesus' birth was also the time during which Caesar Augustus issued a decree that all the world would be taxed. This is the reason that Joseph took his wife, who was large with child, to Bethlehem thus fulfilling prophecy.[57] They were among many individuals who had to travel long distances to the towns and cities of their origin in order to pay this tax. It would be imprudent for Caesar Augustus to require that Rome's subjects travel to pay such a duty during the middle of winter. One of the first recorded references to the date of Christ's birth was made in approximately 200 A.D. by Clement of Alexandria who stated the following:

> "There are those who have determined not only the year of our Lord's birth, but also the day;

---

[56] Luke 2:8-11.
[57] Luke 2:1, Micah 5:1-2

and they say that it took place in the 28th year of Augustus, and in the 25th day of (the Egyptian month) Pachon (May 20 in our calendar)...And treating of His Passion, with very great accuracy, some say that it took place in the 16th year of Tiberius, on the 25th of Phamenoth [March 21]; and others on the 25th of Pharmuthi (April 21) and others say that on the 19th of Pharmuthi (April 15) the Savior suffered. Further, others say that He was born on the 24th or 25th of Pharmuthi (April 20 or 21)."[58]

Apparently, there was no consensus regarding the birth of the Messiah. In addition, out of all the proposed birthdates of Christ, December 25th is not mentioned. So, if the specific date of Christ' birth is not stated in Scripture, if the Scriptural evidence we do have points us to an earlier time of the year, and if about two hundred years later the birth of Christ was a point of contention, how was December 25th chosen as the Savior's birth date? This date is perplexing unless one understands the significance of this specific date and the time surrounding the winter solstice for pagans. One must also keep in mind the Roman Church's willingness to wink at and even encourage pagan practices and feasts to bring the heathens into the fold. In 274, Emperor Aurelian made the cult of Sol Invictus ("Invincible Sun") an official cult in Rome. It is less clear if Sol Invictus was an entirely new version of the cult of Sol or a revival of the cult of Elagabalus.

---

[58] Clement, *Stromateis* 1.21.145.

Nevertheless, on December 25, the day of the winter solstice, of the same year Aurelian inaugurated a temple to Sol.[59] So, to supplant the worship of the "Unconquerable Sun" Pope Julius and Catholic leaders declared December 25th as the official birth date of Christ. In 336 A.D. we find the first recorded celebration of Christmas in a list of Catholic Bishops which reads, "25 Dec: natus Christus in Betleem Judeae."[60]

Saturnalia, Brumalia, & Mithraism

The Saturnalia was an ancient Roman festival that lasted for seven days (December 17-24). During Saturnalia roles were reversed. In honor of Saturn slaves ate before, ruled over, and disrespected their masters. During Saturnalia gambling, drunkenness, and sexual licentiousness was prevalent. At certain times in history, Saturnalia also consisted of human sacrifice. The "king" or "lord of misrule" of the Saturnalia was chosen from among the enemies of Rome by lots and dressed in the insignia of Kronos. He was forced to take part in gluttony and debauchery and then sacrificed at the conclusion of the festival. Saturnalia was capped by the Brumalia (December 25). The birth of Mithras (Persian) was also celebrated on December 25th. In 354 Liberius commanded that Christ' birth be observed on the 25th of December to counteract these observances. The names of these pagan festivals died but the

---

[59] *Chronography* of 354.
[60] December 25th, Christ born in Bethlehem, Judea.

spirit survived within the Christmas celebration. This is evidenced by the most popular Christmas rites and symbols (e.g. the suspension of work, feasting, gift giving, decking homes with evergreens, lighting candles, and caroling).

Ave, Caesar! Io, Saturnalia! (Sir Lawrence Alma-Tadema - 1880)

THE PAGAN ORIGINS OF CHRISTIAN HOLIDAYS

Relief of Mithras the bull slayer

Christmas Symbols
Mistletoe

It is Christian tradition to hang mistletoe over doorways. The mistletoe is a parasitic plant that was considered sacred by the Druids. The ancient Druids believed that mistletoe possessed healing and magical powers. Pliny writes, "The Druids- that is what they call their magicians - hold nothing more sacred than mistletoe and a tree on which it is growing... Mistletoe is rare, and when found, it is gathered with great ceremony, and particularly on the sixth day of the moon."[61] It was also believed that the plant possessed fertility attributes. The white berries symbolized the divine semen of God and the red berries of the holly represented the goddess' menstrual blood.[62] It is unclear of exactly when kissing under the mistletoe began; but it is probable that the custom is associated with the bough's perceived fertility.

Yule Log

According to Babylonian tradition, Tammuz was the reincarnation of Nimrod. This process of death and reincarnation was represented by a log and a tree. The Yule log that was set ablaze represented the death of Nimrod. The next day a tree was used to symbolize the rebirth of Nimrod through Tammuz. Yule was a winter solstice

---

[61] Pliny, *Natural History, XVI*, 95.
[62] Gerina Dunwich, *Wicca Craft: The Book of Herbs, Magick, and Dreams* (New York: Citadel Press, 1991), 35.

festival that was also celebrated by the peoples of Northern Europe. During Yule a log was meticulously chosen. Parts of the Yule log were lit for twelve days, and each day a different sacrifice was made. In honor of the Scandinavian fertility deity Jule pagans kept a log ablaze for twelve days. This is the precursor of the twelve days of Christmas between Christmas and Epiphany.

Christmas Trees

The Christmas tree is probably the most recognized Christmas symbol. But, since antiquity pagans have used trees that remain green annually as objects of worship. In Egypt, pagans decked their homes with palm trees during the time of the winter solstice in honor of Ra. In honor of Saturn the Romans decorated their homes with evergreen boughs during Saturnalia. Tree worship was even practiced in China. This custom was also practiced by converts to Catholicism. The ecclesiastical writer Tertullian even complained that too many Christians decorated their homes as the heathens did during their festivals. The modern Christmas tree tradition, however, derived from Germany. It is believed that the Protestant reformer Martin Luther began the tradition of adding lighted candles to evergreens. It was also the Germans who brought the custom to the Americas. However, many Americans viewed the Christmas tree as a pagan remnant. Early Americans were correct in their assessment that placing a tree in one's home is pagan. Jeremiah writes:

> Hear ye the word which the Lord speaketh unto you, O house of Israel: Thus saith the Lord, Learn not the way of the heathen, and be not dismayed at the signs of heaven; for the heathen are dismayed at them. For the customs of the people are vain: for one cutteth a tree out of the forest, the work of the hands of the workman, with the axe. They deck it with

silver and with gold; they fasten it with nails and with hammers, that it move not.[63]

Santa Claus

The mythical figure known today as Santa Claus has developed over a number of years and is a combination of figures such as the historical Nicholas of Myra, Sinterklaas, Father Christmas, the Germanic god Odin, as well as American commercialism. The inspiration of Santa Claus comes in part from the 4th Century Catholic bishop Nicholas of Myra (present day Demre). According to legend, Nicholas was known for doing miracles and giving gifts to the impoverished. Supposedly, his most generous act was providing dowries for young women that saved them from a life of prostitution. In some European countries, mainly Northern Italy and regions of Austria, gifts and sweet treats are distributed to children on St. Nicholas' Day (December 6). There are also obvious parallels between Odin and Santa Claus. In Norse mythology Odin (Woden) is associated with magic, war, hunting, and is also the father of Thor. Prior to the rise of Christianity, when yuletide was widely celebrated it was believed that supernatural occurrences were widespread. One of these was the Wild Hunt. During this procession Odin rode an eight legged horse named Sleipner.[64] Sleipner is

---

[63] Jeremiah 10:1-4.
[64] There are also similarities with Thor who according to legend rode a chariot pulled by two reindeer named Gnasher and Cracker.

likened to the eight original reindeer of Santa due to his ability to leap across the night sky.[65] The narrative associated with Santa's gift giving is also similar to Odin's. As children waited for a visit from Odin, they put food (carrots, straw, and sugar) in their boots and placed them near the chimney for Sleipner to eat. Odin rewarded the children with gifts.

In Luxembourg, Belgium, and the Netherlands Saint Nicholas (Sinterklass) is portrayed as an old man with a long beard and canonical robes who has a book in which he keeps track of children's acts and gives them gifts based on whether they have been naughty or nice. In some Alpine countries a frightening looking creature called Krampus scares and punishes children who are wayward during the year.

---

[65] Initially, there were only eight reindeer. Rudolph the Red-Nosed Reindeer, the ninth reindeer, appeared for the first time in a 1939 booklet written by Robert L. May that was published by Montgomery Ward.

THE PAGAN ORIGINS OF CHRISTIAN HOLIDAYS

Father Christmas riding a goat

"Merry Old Santa Claus" illustration by Thomas Nast
that appeared in Harper's Weekly January 1, 1881

Christmas card with Krampus

Depiction of St. Nicholas and Krampus in Austria (Winter 1896)

In England there was Father Christmas. He was portrayed as a jolly large bearded man with green or scarlet clothing lined in fur, riding a goat, and assisted by elves instead of Krampus. When England abandoned the feast day of Saint Nicholas (December 6) the Father Christmas celebration was transferred to December 25th to coincide with Christmas. In the English speaking world Sinterklass, St. Nicholas, and Father Christmas merged. In the United States the word "Sinterklaas" was Americanized into Santa Claus, and first appeared in the American press in 1773.[66] Initially, his canonical attire was replaced with a green winter coat and he was depicted as a portly Dutch sailor. The poem "A Visit From St. Nicholas" (better known as "Twas the Night Before Christmas") by Clement Clarke Moore solidified many of the modern attributes of Santa Claus which include riding on a sleigh and landing on the roofs of homes, entering the chimney with a sack of toys, and reindeer named Dasher, Dancer, Prancer, Vixen, Comet, Cupid, Dunder, and Blixem. The image of Santa as a rotund bearded man was popularized by the American cartoonist Thomas Nast in an 1863 illustration that appeared in Harper's Weekly. In the early 20th century images of Santa were used by companies such as White Rock Beverages. However, the Coca Cola Company has influenced the modern depiction of Santa a great deal. For instance, the popular 1930's Coca Cola Christmas depiction by Haddon Sunblom of Santa Claus donning red and white, is largely

---

[66] Rivington's Gazette (New York City), December 23, 1773.

why Santa Claus is almost exclusively depicted today wearing these two colors.

Christmas is undoubtedly rooted in paganism and those who observe celebrations do so in error. Again, Jesus could not have been born on December 25th. The choosing of this day was a strategic maneuver by the Roman Church. Furthermore, even if Jesus was born on December 25th God never commanded that we commemorate his birth. The Christmas rituals, symbols, and figures are merely remnants of the pagan rituals, symbols, and figures of old. Even the word "Christmas", which comes from the words "Christ" and "mass", is erroneous because Christ never had a mass. The round wafer used during the Catholic mass is a symbol associated with pagan sun worship, which is actually at the root of the Christmas festival. Knowing all of this how can one possibly substantiate the observance of Christmas and simultaneously profess to be a follower of Christ?

12
SHINING THE LIGHT ON EPIPHANY

Blessing of Waters (Vodokrst) in Skopje, Macedonia in the 1920's

Despite the obscure origins of Epiphany it is indeed pagan in origin. The festival of Epiphany has been present in the Christian Orthodox Church since the end of the third century. Epiphany refers to the day but also the season that follows. It ends when the season of Lent begins, and has always been the celebration of the appearance of God. The Greek words ἐπιφάνεια, epiphaneia (appearance, manifestation), Θεοφάνεια, theophaneia (the divine manifestation, appearance) and phota (lights), "festival of lights", "the day of lights", or "the twelfth day of Christmas" are traditionally used to name this feast. It supposedly commemorates the following events:

1. Magi (wise men of the East) visited the infant Jesus
2. The baptism of Jesus in the Jordan River
3. Jesus turned water to wine at a wedding at Cana

When light is shed upon this festival it like other Christian holidays is rooted in paganism and contrary to the Holy Scriptures.

The word "epiphany" originates from the word associated with the appearance of a pagan god or goddess in a vision.[67] Epiphany predates the December 25th Christmas celebration. Clement of Alexandria (150-215 AD) was the first to mention a celebration of an appearance of God in relation to Jesus' baptism. He stated that it was observed by the Basilidian Gnostics: "The disciples of Basilides[68] celebrate the day of his baptism as well, spending

---

[67] Prudence Jones and Nigel Pennick, *A History of Pagan Europe* (London: Routledge, 1995), 76.
[68] Clement, *Stromateis*, I, xxi, 45.

the previous night in reading. They say it was the fifteenth year of Tiberius Caesar, the fifteenth of the month Tybi; but some say the eleventh of the same month."[69] It is likely that they also commemorated Christ' birth because they held the belief, as did the Cerinthians, that a divine Christ descended in the form of a dove upon the human Jesus at the time of his baptism. Ammianus Marcellinus (330-395 AD) provides us with the first mention of Epiphany in secular literature which reads, "And in order to conceal this[70] for a time, on the festival that Christians celebrate the Epiphany, he entered their church, prayed to their deity in the usual way, and departed." While it is not entirely clear how it happened, the dominant view is that the Epiphany festival originated in the East, and by the 4th century was well established within Eastern Christianity. John Cassian (ca. 360-after 430) stated that in Egypt the festival of Epiphany had a twofold purpose:

> In the province of Egypt there is a custom preserved by ancient tradition that, when the day of Epiphany is over, which the priests of that region designated as the day of the Lord's baptism as well as of his birth according to the flesh, and so they observe it as the festival of both mysteries, not separately as in the western districts, but during a single celebration of this day, Alexandrian patriarch sends letters throughout all the churches of Egypt, by which

---

[69] The eleventh of the Egyptian month Tybi is January 6.
[70] refers to his conversion to paganism

he fixes the beginning of Lent and the day for Easter, not only for all the cities, but also all the monasteries. Epiphany was first celebrated within eastern Christianity.[71]

According to Clement January 6 or 10 was the day that the Festival of Epiphany was celebrated. It is likely that the Basilides chose the date that was consistent with the time of the blessing of the Nile River in Egypt. The Eastern Roman Church was the first to observe Epiphany as the birth date of Christ. The Roman churches of the West observed the nativity of Christ on December 25th. According to the bishop of Cyrus Panarium of Epiphanius, who as a child spent time in the monasteries of Egypt, January 6 corresponded with the birth of the pagan god Aeon. He writes:

> In many places they celebrated a very great festival on the night of Epiphany, particularly in the so-called Koreion at Alexandria. There is an immense temple there, the temenos of Kore. After watching all night, singing and playing the flute in honor of the sacred image (Kore), and celebrating a pannychis, they go down after cock crow, bearing torches into a kind of underground crypt, carrying up a carved wooden idol, who sits naked on a bier and has a cruciform seal on his forehead, two more on his hands, and two more on his knees, altogether five gold seals. They carry the god seven times around the center of the temple amid loud

---

[71] John Cassian, Collationes 10, 2.

playing of flutes and drums and singing of hymns, and then carry it to this underground place. When they are asked what mystery this is, they say that at this hour Kore—that is the Virgin—has given birth to Aeon."[72]

By the 300's Epiphany observance was widespread throughout the Eastern part of the Catholic Church. Epiphany eventually became more closely associated with the birth of Christ. In 353-354 Pope Liberius officially ordered the observance of the nativity of Christ on December 25th.[73] It is likely that Epiphany observance on January 6 as well as on December 25 was associated with the paganism.

The Catholic Church did not obliterate pagan practices, but rather adopted them, which is the case for the Epiphany celebration. There is no record that the apostles commemorated the birth of Christ, neither was this the practice during the New Testament Church. Origen writes:

> Of all the holy people in the Scriptures, no one is recorded to have kept a feast or held a great banquet on his birthday. It is only sinners who make great rejoicings over the day in which they were born into this world.[74]

---

[72] *Panarion*, 51, 22 8ff.: II, 285, 10ff.

[73] Constantine I introduced the celebration of December 25th as the birth of Christ, however, Christians largely associated this day with paganism. Throughout much of Rome December 25th was celebrated in by the Sun cults.

[74] Origen, *Homilies on Leviticus*.

Jesus could not have been born on January 6 or December 25. Furthermore there is no commandment found in the Holy Scriptures to observe Epiphany. All those who light candles on in observance of Epiphany in actuality dwell in spiritual darkness.

Clement of Alexandria (c. 150- c.215)

Pope Liberius (?-366)

13
FEASTS IN HONOR OF THE QUEEN OF HEAVEN

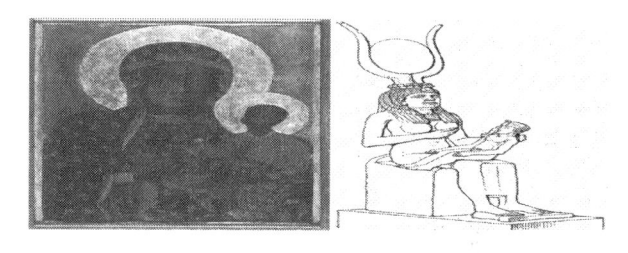

"In all seriousness- without meaning to be frivolous- without meaning to be irreverent, and more than all, without meaning to be blasphemous, - I state as my simple deduction from the things I have seen and the things I have heard, that the Holy Personages rank thus in Rome:

> First- "The Mother of God"- otherwise the Virgin Mary.
> Second- The Deity.
> Third- Peter.
> Fourth- Some twelve or fifteen canonized Popes and martyrs.
> Fifth- Jesus Christ the Savior- (but always as an

infant in arms.)"
  -*The Innocents Abroad*, Mark Twain 1869, p. 306.

In Christianity, Mary is held in high regard. In various Christian denominations, and particularly within Catholicism, Mary is actually worshipped on the same plane as God. Those Christian denominations that worship Mary have bestowed blasphemous titles upon her such as the "Queen of Heaven" "Mediatrix" and the "Mother of God". In addition to this position and titles equal with God there are many celebrations in honor of Mary called Marian Feasts. It is true that Mary was a servant of God; she was blessed and highly favored. But nowhere in the Scriptures do we read that a special status is to be given to Mary and certainly not a position equal to that of God. To hold feasts in her honor and refer to her as the "Queen of Heaven", or the "Mediatrix" between God and man, and to attribute to her the spiritual title "Mother of God" is simply not Biblical. On the contrary if we look closely we find that the veneration of Mary is not only apostasy but is also a continuation of the worship of the pagan goddesses of antiquity. Before examining the festivals dedicated to Mary it is first necessary to analyze the titles and position that has been bestowed upon her.

Blasphemous Titles Attributed to Mary

The Mother of God

At the Ecumenical Council of Ephesus in 431 A.D. Mary was officially given the title "Mother of

God". This allowed the pagans to continue the worship of their mother goddesses. After the decline of paganism, Mary was worshipped as the most prominent manifestation of the divine feminine.[75] One of the earliest churches dedicated to Mary the "Mother of God" was built on the site of a temple dedicated to Diana.[76] Another replaced the temple of Isis in Soissons. The term "Mother of God" once used to refer to the Egyptian goddess Isis was transferred to Mary. In the Lateran Council of 469 it was declared that anyone who does not declare that Mary is indeed the mother of God should be condemned.

Mediatrix

Another title that has been bestowed upon Mary is Mediatrix (Theotokos). In Roman Catholic Mariology this is the belief that Mary is the mediator in salvific redemption by Jesus. This title was attributed to Mary as early as the 4th century. Eprhaem the Syrian calls her "after the mediator, you (Mary) are the mediatrix of the world".[77] Because of her relationship with Jesus Christ, the mediation of Mary was considered paramount in comparison to the intercession of saints. However, according to the New Testament the only mediator

---

[75] Murphy Pizza and James R. Lewis, *Handbook of Contemporary Paganism: Vol. 2 of Brill Handbooks on Contemporary Religion* (The Netherlands: Brill Handbooks on Contemporary Religion, 2009), 336.
[76] Prudence Jones and Nigel Pennick, *A History of Pagan Europe* (London: Routledge, 1995), 75.
[77] Ephraem, Oratio IV, *Ad Deiparam*.

between God and man is the Messiah. The following verses concerning Christ's mediation affirm this:

> "For there is one God and one mediator between God and men, the man Christ Jesus, who gave himself as a ransom for all to be testified in due time."[78]
>
> "Wherefore he (Jesus) is able to save them to the uttermost that come unto God by him, seeing he ever liveth to make intercession for them."[79]
>
> "In whom (Jesus) we have boldness and access with confidence by the faith of him."[80]

Furthermore, the term "Mediatrix" is a pagan term that was attributed to Mylitta, the Mother Goddess of Babylon and should not be attributed to Mary.

Queen of Heaven

Another title that has been given to Mary is the "Queen of Heaven". The tradition of referring to Mary as the Queen of Heaven is a long one. However, since antiquity this is a title that has been used to refer to several goddesses. Isis, Anat, Innana, Astarte, Hera, Asherah, and Juno were worshipped under this title. The worship of the

---

[78] I Timothy 2:5-6.
[79] Hebrews 7:25.
[80] Ephesians 3:12.

Queen of Heaven was also recorded in the book of Jeremiah. The prophet writes, "The children gather wood, and the fathers kindle the fire, and the women knead their dough, to make cakes to the queen of heaven, and to pour out drink offerings unto other gods, that they may provoke me to anger."[81] The nation of Israel had fallen so far from God that they believed that their prosperity as a nation was dependent on the worship of this queen. After Jeremiah rebuked their false worship they replied:

> As for the word that thou hast spoken unto us in the name of the Lord, we will not hearken unto thee. But we will certainly do whatsoever thing goeth forth out of our own mouth, to burn incense unto the queen of heaven, and to pour out drink offerings unto her, as we have done, we, and our fathers, our kings, and our princes, in the cities of Judah, and in the streets of Jerusalem: for then had we plenty of victuals, and were well and saw no evil. But since we left off to burn incense to the queen of heaven, and to pour out drink offerings unto her, we have wanted all things, and we have been consumed by the sword and by the famine.[82]

This pagan title has simply been ascribed to Mary so that mother goddess mother can continue under the name of Mary. Since in the Christian

---

[81] Jeremiah 7:18.
[82] It is probable that in this instance Israel was worshiping the goddess Astarte.

religion Mary has replaced the pagan goddesses of old it is easy to understand how she is now worshiped. There are many feasts that are observed in honor of Mary. The following are the most prominent Marian feast days.

January 1	Mary, Mother of God
January 8	Our Lady of Prompt
February 2	Purification of the Virgin
February 11	Our Lady of Lourdes
March 25	Annunciation
April 26	Our Lady of Good Counsel
May 1	Queen of Heaven
May 13	Our Lady of Fatima
May 24	Mary Help of Christians
May 31	Visitation of the Blessed Virgin Mary
June 27	Our Lady of Perpetual Help
July 16	Our Lady of Mount Carmel
August 2	Our Lady of Angels
August 5	Dedicaiton of the Basilica of St. Mary Major
August 15	Assumption into Heaven
August 21	Our Lady of Knock
August 22	Queenship of Mary
August 22	Black Madonna of Czestochowa
August 31	The Virgin Mary Mediatrix
September 8	Nativity of the Blessed Virgin Mary
September 12	The Most Holy Name of the Blessed Virgin Mary
September 15	Our Lady of Sorrows

September 19	Our Lady of La Salette
September 24	Our Lady of Walsingham, Feast of Our Lady of Ransom
October 7	Most Holy Rosary
November 16	Our Lady of Mercy
November 21	Presentation of Mary
December 8	Immaculate Conception
December 12	Our Lady of Guadalupe
1 Day after Ascension of Jesus	Our Lady of the Apostles
1 Day after Pentecost	Our Lady of Holy Church
9 Days after Corpus Christi	Immaculate Heart of Mary

Mariology, the worship of Mary, is simply the continuation of pagan mother goddess worship. It is another compromise with paganism by Catholicism. Through this veneration of Mary, numerous festivals and celebrations have emerged in her honor. However, such veneration was discouraged by Jesus. The words of Jesus, the true Intercessor, Son of God, and King, enlighten us concerning whether or not we should engage in Mary veneration and hold feasts in her honor. The Gospel according to Luke reads:

> And it came to pass, as he spake these things, a certain woman of the company lifted up her voice, and said unto him, Blessed is the womb that bare thee, and the paps which though hast sucked. But he (Jesus) said, Yea rather, blessed are they that hear the word of God, and keep

it."[83]

Isis, also known as the "Queen of Heaven"

---

[83] Luke 11:27-28.

Diana of Versailles, also referred to as the Queen of Heaven

Coronacion de la Virgen, Diego Velaquez, 1645

14
GOD IS A SPIRIT

Why is it wrong to observe "Christianized" holidays such as Christmas and Easter? Some would argue that simply because holidays are rooted in paganism does not mean that it is wrong for Christians to observe them. And, it is acceptable to observe holidays as long as these days are celebrated in the name of God. However, such a stance is erroneous because, "God is a Spirit and they that worship him, must worship him in spirit and in truth." The truth is that Jesus was not born on December 25th; nor was the Messiah resurrected on Easter Sunday. So how can we worship Him according to a lie and expect Him to be pleased. Furthermore, the Almighty God has already established holy days that we are to observe. Man's holidays only point backward to their pagan origin, but all of God's holy days are "a shadow of things to come" The feasts of God outline the plan of salvation for all of mankind. These holy days are as follows:

Seventh Day Sabbath
Passover
Feast of Unleavened Bread
Pentecost (Feast of Weeks)
Memorial of the Blowing of Trumpets
Day of Atonement
Feast of Tabernacles

So, how can one replace the feast days that God has established to celebrate festivals that include rituals that are contrary to God in every aspect except for in name? Those who do so have made the commandment of God of none effect with pagan traditions. Individuals who celebrate Christian holidays, draw near to God with their mouth, and honor God through words, however, their mind is far from God. And, their worship of God is in vain. At least the pagan has no qualms about the worship in which he engages. But, the Christian of today practices paganism in the name of Christ. Understand, to be a true Christian means to be a follower of Christ. Christ observed the feast days, as did Paul, the Apostles, early Christians, and true Christians today. During the millennial reign of Christ he will reestablish proper worship on the earth, and those who overlook His feasts will suffer severe consequences. Zechariah writes:

> And it shall come to pass, ever one that is left of all the nations which came against Jerusalem

shall even go up from year to year to worship the King, the Lord of hosts, and the keep the feasts of tabernacles. And it shall be, that whoso will not come up of all the families of the earth unto Jerusalem to worship the King, the Lord of hosts, even upon them shall be no rain. And if the family of Egypt go not up, and come not, that have no rain; there shall be the plague, wherewith the Lord will smite the heathen that come not up to keep the feasts of tabernacles. This shall be the punishment of Egypt, and the punishment off all nations that come not up to keep the feast of tabernacles.[84]

Question- After Christ returns why are the earth's inhabitants observing the same holy days that are written about in the Old Testament? Answer- Jesus Christ the same yesterday, and today, and forever. The holy days of the Lord were good yesterday, are still good today, and will be so tomorrow. In order to be a true Christian one must abandon pagan holidays and observe the feast days of God. And when opposition for doing so comes, (and it surely will) just remember the following words Paul wrote to the Colossians, "Let no man therefore judge you in meat, or in drink, or in respect of an holyday, or of the new moon, or of the sabbath days: Which are a shadow of things to come; but the body is of Christ." (Colossians 2:16-17).

---

[84] Zechariah 14:16-18.

BIBLIOGRAPHY

Aleksandrovich, Aleksander. *History of the Byzantine Empire, 324-1453 Vol. 1*. Madison: University of Wisconsin, 1952.

Blavatsky, Helens Petrovna. *The Theosophical Glossary*. New York: Theosophical Publishing Society, 1892.

Bonwick, James. *Egyptian Belief and Modern Thought*. London: C. Kegan Paul & Co., 1878.

Burchett, Bessie Rebecca. *Janus In Roman Life and Cult: A Study in Roman Religions*. Menasha, WI: George Banta Publishing, Co., 1912.

Cassian, John. *Conference 21, The First Conference of Abbot Theonas on the Relaxation During the Fifty Days*, Chapter 30.

Catechism of the Catholic Church, 1376.

Chronography of 354.

Clement, *Stromateis*, I, xxi.

Codex Justinianus. Lib. 3, tit, 12, 3.

Daniels, Cora Linn Morrison and Charles McClellan Stevens. *Encyclopedia of Superstitions, Folklore, and the Occult Sciences of the World*. Milwaukee, WI.:J.H. Yewdale & Sons Co., 1903.

Drew, A.J. *A Wiccan Bible: Exploring the Mysteries of the Craft from Birth to Summerland*. Franklin Lakes, NJ: Career Press, 2003.

Dunwhich, Gerina. *Wicca Craft: The Book of Herbs, Magick, and Dreams*. New York: Citadel Press, 1991.

Durant, William. *The Age of Faith: The Story of Civilization Vol. 4*, New York: Simon and

Schuster, 1950.

Eason, Cassandra. *A Complete Guide to Night Magic*. New York: Kensington Publishing Corp, 2003.

Ephraem, Oratio IV, *Ad Deiparam*.

Frazier, James George. *The Golden Bough: A Study in Magic and Religion* (London: Macmillan and Company, 1912.

Gibbon, Edward. *The History of the Decline and Fall of the Roman Empire*. London: Oxford University Press,1837.

------. *History of Christianity*. New York: Peter Eckler Publishing Co.,1916.

Gibbons, James. *The Faith of Our Fathers: Being a Plain Exposition and Vindication of the Church Founded by Our Lord Jesus Christ*. New York: John Murphy Company Publishers, 1917.

Gildea, William L. *Paschale Gaudium* in The Catholic World, Vol. LVIII., No. 348. New York: Office of The Catholic World, March 1894.

Grimassi, Raven. *Encyclopedia of Wicca and Witchcraft.* St. Paul: MN: Llewellyn Publications, 2000.

Grolier Publishing Company. *The New Book of Knowledge.* Danbury, CT: Grolier Publishing Company, 1981.

Hall, Manly, P. *The Secret Teachings of the Ages: An Encyclopedia Outline of Masonic, Hermetic, Qabbalistic and Rosicrucian Symbolic Philosophy*. San Francisco: H.S. Crocker Co., Inc., 1928.

Holzmann, Heinrich Julius. *Kanon und Tradition:*

ein Beitrag zur neueren Dogmengeschichte und Symbolik. Ludwigsburg, Germany: F. Reihm, 1859.

Herodotus and Alfred Denis Godley, *The Histories Volume 1*. London: William Heineman, 1920.

Holy Bible King James Version.

Jackson, Samuel Macauley. *The New Schaff-Herzog Encyclopedia of Religious Knowledge*, New York: Funk & Wagnalls Co., 1909.

Jones, Prudence and Pennick Nigel. *A History of Pagan Europe*. London: Routledge, 1995.

McCoy, Edain. *The Sabbats: A Witch's Approach to Living the Old Ways*, St. Paul, MN: Llewellyn Publications, 1994.

Origen, *Homilies on Leviticus.*

Ovid, Nagle, Betty Rose. *Ovid's Fasti: Roman Holidays*. Bloomington, IN: Indiana University Press, 1995.

Papal Bull Transiturus de hoc mundo.

Pizza, Murphy and Lewis, James R. *Handbook of Contemporary Paganism: Vol. 2 of Brill Handbooks on Contemporary Religion* The Netherlands: Brill Handbooks on Contemporary Religion, 2009.

Pliny. *Natural History*, XVI.

Panarion, 51, 22 8ff.: II, 285, 10ff.

Reader's Digest. *The Last Two Million Years*. London: The Reader's Digest Association, 1973.

Rivington's Gazette (New York City), December 23, 1773.

Rudwin, Maximilian Josef. *The Origin of the German Carnival*. New York: The G.E.

Stechert & Co., 1920.

Sermon, William. *The Ladies Companion, or the English Midwife*. London, 1671.

Schaff, Philip and Henry Wace. *A Select Library of Nicene and Post- Nicene Fathers of the Christian Church Second Series, Vol. XI*. New York: The Christian Literature Company, 1894.

Sermon, William. *The Ladies Companion, or the English Midwife.* London: Printed for Edward Thomas, 1671.

Shakespeare, William. *The Dramatic Works of William Shakespeare, with a Glossary*, London: H.G. Bohn, 1858.

Smith, William George and Anthon, Charles *A Dictionary of Greek and Roman and Antiquities.*, Harper, 1870

Walsh, William Shepard. *Curiosities of Popular Customs and of Rites, Ceremonies, Observances, and Miscellaneous Antiquities*. Philadelphia: J.B. Lippincott Co., 1898.

INTO EGYPT AGAIN WITH SHPS: A MESSAGE TO THE FORGOTTEN ISRAELITES (AFRICAN AMERICANS)
Elisha J. Israel©

NOW AVAILABLE ON-LINE @ ELISHAJISRAEL.COM, AMAZON.COM, & BARNESANDNOBLE.COM

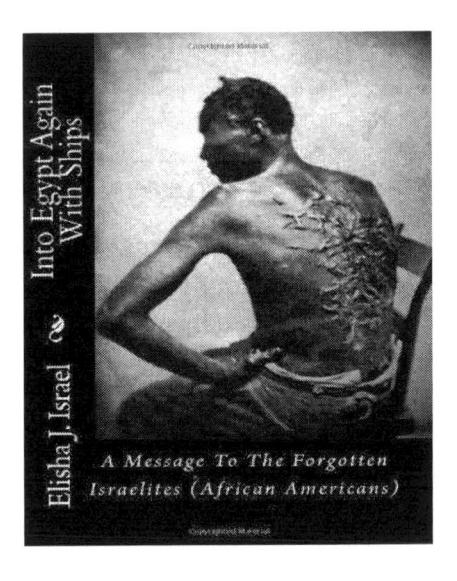

INTO EGYPT AGAIN WITH SHIPS explains the spiritual implications regarding more that 250 years of chattel slavery, 100 years of Jim Crow, semi-permanent underclass status, and loss of true identity that "African Americans" have suffered in the United States. This book also reveals the biblical solution that will lead to the complete liberation of a people. All those who have descended from slaves, and consider themselves to be "Negro", "Black", or "African American" should have the audacity to read this book.

Killing Black Innocents: The Program to Control "African American" Reproduction (from Slavery's End to the Present Day Self-Inflicted Genocide)
Elisha J. Israel

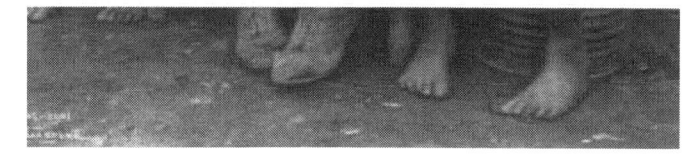

Book Available @ ElishaJIsrael.com, Amazon.com, & BarnesandNoble.com

In ***Killing Black Innocents***, Elisha J. Israel argues that throughout American history there has been an ongoing program to manipulate the rate of African American reproduction. He maintains that during the slavery era there were significant efforts to drastically increase the numbers of slaves through rape and slave breeding for the purpose of monetary gain. Israel goes on to argue that following emancipation the agenda has been to reduce the black population through compulsory sterilization, long-term contraceptives, and abortion. This work unearths a largely buried history of reproduction abuse and in frank terms describes the effects of African American complicity in this program (e.g. approximately a number equivalent to 25% of the black population decimated through abortion). This sobering account not only gives a voice to those who have been exploited by slave masters, medical professionals, and government officials; it is a passionate cry in defense of black innocents.

ABOUT THE AUTHOR

Elisha J. Israel is a minister and educator. He is also the author of Into Egypt Again With Ships: A Message to the Forgotten Israelites (African Americans) and Killing Black Innocents: The Program to Control "African American" Reproduction (from Slavery's End to the Present-Day Self-Inflicted Genocide).

Made in the USA
Lexington, KY
15 September 2019